Fun With
Sticker Book

Lucy Cousins

Take the sticker pages out of the middle of this book.
Open the pages so the stickers and the pictures
in the book can be seen side by side.
Read the words on each page.
Then choose which sticker to peel off
and where to put it in each picture.

CANDLEWICK PRESS
CAMBRIDGE, MASSACHUSETTS

Maisy and Tallulah are flying their kites. Which one is Maisy's?

What else is
in the sky?

Charley and Cyril
are splashing in
the pool.

Can you find
their boat
and ball?

Eddie needs his orange shorts and his missing skates.

Who's riding behind Maisy?

Where are Tallulah's drum and Charley's tape player?

Who is
dancing
with them?

Can you find Maisy and Cyril's sand toys?

Find Eddie's toy rabbit.

Help set the table for a tea party.

Who else is riding
Charley's bike?

Find the basket and
the missing wheel.

Bye-bye, Maisy!